50 Shades of Color

Sensual Sirens

www.ingramcontent.com/pod-product-compliance
Lightning Source LLC
Chambersburg PA
CBHW080646190526
45169CB00009B/3517
9781530795680